MW01251410

HOW TO NETWORK

BUILD INSTANT TRUST & RESPECT WITH ANYONE YOU MEET

TAM PHAM

Your Free Gift

As a way of showing my gratitude for your purchase, I'm offering a free networking guide that's exclusive only to you. These lessons highlight all of the takeaways you've learned in this book and will help you in every aspect of your life. In this free guide, I'll show you how to genuinely connect with people anywhere you go…. You can download this free guide here:

www.TamPham.co/NetworkingBonus

Table of Contents

Intro

In school, no one ever teaches you how to "network." We've been taught to think that we need to meet as many people as possible and shove business cards down their throats in order to create connections. This is the exact opposite of what you want to do.

By the end of this book, you will learn **how to become a badass networker.**

You will be genuinely connecting with people left and right to the point where they will be the ones asking to meet YOU!

Because remember: "It's not what you know or who you know, it's all about who knows you."

My name is Tam and whether you're a...

- Student
- Graduate
- Young Professional
- Creative Artist
- Performer
- Entrepreneur
- Business Executive
- Golden Retriever
- Or a Human Being...

You're in the right place. No matter what you do, networking is CRUCIAL in our lives.

Networking can:

- open doors to opportunities.

- help you share ideas and exchange knowledge.

- increase your connections, leading to higher success

- lead to future collaboration in businesses and projects

- create and strengthen relationships with like-minded people

There are many myths about networking and how it's only used by sleazy marketers... I'm going to debunk these myths and I'm going to give you all the secrets I wish I knew five years ago.

Why am I writing this? This is a book purely to help YOU expand your network and connect with others.

Why should you listen to me? The question I get asked the most is, *"How the hell do you know so many people?"*

Am I super attractive? No.

Am I special? No.

Am I super smart? No.

Am I rich? No.

Am I a famous actor? No.

Am I a drug dealer? No.

Am I a great party host? No.

So how DO you know so many people, Tam?

I have spent my whole life "networking." Through my experiences, research, and diligent practice, I've learned how to get people to like, trust, and respect me.

Because of this, I'm constantly bombarded with opportunities; job offers, free tickets to event, work promotions, and a variety of other benefits.

This is the *magic* that happens when you actively invest in your network... People will want to help you succeed!

I landed one of my dream jobs serving as the Entrepreneurship Director for Camp BizSmart, teaching young people how to start their own businesses at places like Stanford University. How? I met the CEO of Camp BizSmart through a networking conference two years ago and we're not only great friends, but he served as a mentor to me throughout my entrepreneurship journey..

I'm sharing all the secrets that connected me with entrepreneurs, professionals, and new friends, because remember: networking is a SKILL. It is not something you are born with (Trust me, I'm an introvert).

Jacky, a student and aspiring entrepreneur from Silicon Valley says, *"The best thing about this book is that it can be read on Monday, and on Tuesday you're already experiencing the results."*

I PROMISE you that you WILL get results.

Such as...

1) More connections

2) More opportunities

3) More benefits

Guaranteed. If you follow this guide and practice networking consistently, people will be asking to meet YOU for coffee.

If you've read this far, I can tell that you are extremely curious to know what's next. If you're reading this just to consume information… I'm going to call you out. Read this book, use it as a reference, but most importantly…

TAKE ACTION

Do NOT be the kind of person who misses out on new chances & connections.

Be the person who takes advice from someone who's been there before.

Be the person that people would be EAGER to meet.

Be the person others would see and wonder, "How do YOU know so many people?"

Be the person who takes action immediately.

Even if you have NO IDEA how to start networking, this book will fill in that knowledge gap and provide clear steps of action on how to get started.

These networking tips and tricks you're about to read have been proven to create significant results in not just my life, but also in the lives of many others whom I have personally coached. All you have to do is keep reading each chapter, take notes, and follow through with action!

Each chapter will give you new insights on how to become a better networker.

So grab a notebook, a pen, and a drink. Maybe two.

And let's dive in on how to genuinely connect with people and build a massive network.

Networking Debunked

"Just go network!"

"Tam, you should go out there and network with people."

"Network, network, network..."

Everyone is telling me to go network but WTF DOES THAT MEAN? Does that mean I have to suck up to people so they can like me?

When I was 17, I thought networking was asking, "What do you do?", and listening to people's elevator pitch before giving yours. Then you would exchange business cards... and that's it. When I started doing that, I thought, "YAY! I'M NETWORKING!!!"

I remember coming home with 10 business cards. YESSS, I thought. I followed up with each one of them because I thought that was what you were "supposed to do", but guess what? None of them replied, even to this day.

CURSE YOU!!! They're just haters, I told myself.

But I was wrong. The point of going to an event is not to come home with business cards. The point of networking is to **genuinely connect with people**, which is something I didn't do.

Ivan Misner, Founder of BNI, has defined networking as:

"The process of developing and activating your relationships to increase your business, enhance your knowledge, expand your sphere of influence or serve the community."

When I read this definition, I thought it was so bo0o0orrrriiingg. It's much easier to think of networking MY way.

My definition of networking = making new friends!

WHHHHHAAATTT!??!?!

You might be thinking, *"Tam... Networking is a professional term and must be used as such. Friends are only for casual occasions. Are you serious!?"*

Let me explain.

What does a friend do? They support you, appreciate you, and want the best for you. You also love your friends and naturally want to help them. Aren't these the same qualities you want from your professional peers as well?

Just think about it.

People assume "professional networking" means shoving business cards down people's throats.

That can work but... that is the loser's approach. Instead of being their "professional acquaintance", why don't you just try and be their FRIEND?

Start off as good buddies just chatting about anything. Business, life, ladies (or guys). The point is that true friends always want the best for you.

For example, if I wanted to get my book published and I met an agent who helps authors sell books, it's a win-win! They help me get published and I pay that person for their services. I sell thousands of books; they makes a commission, WIN-WIN.

Or if I wanted to get into marketing and I met a person who was also into marketing. We can collaborate, share ideas, and give feedback to each other on our marketing plans. WIN-WIN.

If I want to date a cute girl and a girl wanted to date a cute guy (like me? you be the judge), then us getting together would be a WIN-WIN ;-)

I'm totally joking by the way.

Is everything always going to be WIN-WIN?

No, it's not. And this is the biggest mistake that 90% of people make (I made up that statistic).

Get out of the mindset that it has to be all uptight and business-like. We're all human beings. Why do we have to act a different way to "build our network?"

Keep this in mind as you read the rest of the book.

Start With YOU

When I used to think of networking, I assumed you had to be extremely extroverted. That you **had** to say hi to everyone in the room and be super "out there."

That is simply not the case.

Before we start ANYTHING with networking, I want to start with YOU. No, nothing is wrong with you. I just want you to promise yourself this:

Promise yourself that you will always be authentic in everything that you do.

Networking is all about genuinely connecting with others... So if you're not authentic, how can you even be on the same level?

"Ok Tam, what the hell does being genuine or authentic mean? That's the worst advice ever."

Being genuine or authentic means **NOT TRYING TO BE SOMEBODY ELSE.** Don't try to be the ultra-extroverted person in the room if you normally don't act that way. Just be YOU.

When people "network", they often put on this mask that is soOoOoOo fake.

People can see it from 10 miles away. Maybe even 20.

The point is, people can SENSE inauthenticity. As human beings, we have a friend or foe mentality. Meaning when we first meet someone, we instinctively think whether we should trust them or not.

While you're networking, don't position yourself to act a certain way just because you think that will get people to like you. Remember, we're making friends! It's supposed to be fun and natural. So relax.

In short, just be you. The world needs YOU.

YOU are awesome :-)

The Decision

One of the biggest challenges with networking isn't going to be money or lack of opportunities... YOU will be your biggest challenge.

I'm going to be honest. I'm an introvert and I constantly used that as an excuse to not meet people. There are going to be SO many reasons why YOU won't want to go to network.

- You don't like talking to people.

- You're shy, awkward, and nervous.

- You think you're going to say something stupid.

- You think you're not going to say anything at all.

- You think they might call you out on how you look.

And so on.

Regardless of what your fear is, be it you're extroverted, introverted, or shy, we must change this mindset. We must make a decision to work towards becoming superb networkers.

I want YOU, right now... to DECIDE that you will build a strong network.

This sounds silly, but let me explain.

I was never a good runner. I used to have breathing problems while growing up. I would constantly overeat and get fatigued extremely fast. For some strange reason, my friend Nancy challenged me to run a half marathon. I told her:

"I'm not a runner."

She asked me if I have ever ran before.

"Yeah, I guess."

"Then you are a runner. You're not a good runner, so learn how to run faster and practice."

Huh, that makes sense.

So after 5 months of training, I ran my first half marathon a few months ago (May 2015) in under 2 hours. That's 13 miles at a 9 minute per mile pace, **INSANE!**

How did I do it? First, I had to tell myself, I am a runner.

I want you to remember this quote:

"If you want to be, do."

My goal was to be a fast runner. So all my actions after that followed towards that bigger picture goal.

- I started eating frequent small meals full of proteins, vegetables, and fruits

- I started training 4 times a week

- I started to reduce the amount of fast food I would normally get

- I started to get excited about running (even when I was never a runner)

- I started to feel more confident about achieving my goal

So how does this relate to you?

If you want to be a superb networker...

DECIDE THAT YOU WILL BE A SUPERB NETWORKER

I don't care if you're inexperienced, "awkward", or an introvert. THOSE ARE ALL EXCUSES.

Let me ask you a question, Have you ever made friends with anyone before?

Yes? Then you know how to network.

All you need is practice. Just like how I "wasn't a runner," these are all skills that can be improved with the right strategies and practice. DECIDE that you will be a superb networker and all the smaller details will follow.

When you're at an event and you're contemplating whether you should join a circle of people, think: What would a superb networker do?

This applies to anything in life.

An average person would say,

"I'm not really good at talking to people so I don't want to leave my house to go to any event."

On the contrary, a motivated person would say,

"I understand my communication skills aren't great. So I'm going to decide to go out every week and practice talking to people."

See the difference!?

The average person always has excuses. They know they're bad at something; instead of trying to improve it, they avoid it entirely. The motivated person understands that they're not skilled at networking… so they're going to practice and improve themselves.

Which type of person are you?

Right now, I want you to DECIDE that

- You will build a strong network

- You will learn to be a superb networker

- You will desire to know more, do more, and be more.

NO MORE EXCUSES

YOU are a "networker." Are you good yet? Maybe not. Can you drastically improve if you use what you've learned and practice? Hell yes.

Remember: If you want to be, do.

Know Your Why

I like to play basketball every week. Why? Because it's fun and helps me stay in shape.

I like to read books every morning. Why? Because it makes me smarter and stimulates my mind.

I like to meet new people. Why? Because I am happier with friends in my life and they give me a lot of support.

When it comes to networking... What's your WHY!?

When you come to a networking event, you have to know why you are there. Are you looking for a job? Making new friends? Connecting with high level people? Want to learn something new?

Do NOT go to networking events just for the hell of it.

That's like taking a job you don't like, with very little benefit, just for the hell of it. That's like going to college, without any sense of direction or purpose, just for the hell of it. That's like studying Computer Science, a subject that you're not even interested in, just for the hell of it.

WHY DO YOU DO ANYTHING?!?!?

When you go to networking events, have a WHY. Be very clear on why you're there.

When I was a freshman in college, I went to different conferences and networking events looking for my first internship. I was always the youngest kid in the room and I looked like it too.

Check out them braces!!! ;-)

The average person would say,

"I'm too young and I don't belong in this conference full of professionals."

The motivated person would say,

"I understand that people perceive that I'm young. What can I do differently to add value and achieve my WHY!?"

I wasn't even old enough to drink but I managed to meet people at bars, high-end conferences, and many different social events.

By the end of my first conference, I had connected with over fifty different professionals. After following up (something we will talk about later), I received five different job opportunities because they respected my ambition and hustle.

How did I do it? Flip to the next chapter where I'll reveal all of the secrets. Starting with one that almost everyone gets wrong.

The ONE secret to networking that everyone gets wrong

There is one thing that everyone does wrong and it's this: They are ALWAYS thinking, *"What is in it for me?"*

O M G

Are you serious, bro (or gal)?

If everyone else had this mindset, no one would benefit! Because everyone is trying to sell themselves and no one is "buying!" It's like going to a farmer's market with no customers walking around. All you see are the other vendors.

I want you to change this mindset from selling to... drum roll please...

Giving.

Instead of thinking: How can I be their friend so that they can refer me to the hiring manager at their company?

We should switch this mindset to:

- How can I help this person achieve their dreams?

- How can I provide value to them or their company?

- How can I make them say "thank you" to me?

Let me just make one thing clear:

NO ONE CARES ABOUT YOU. ALL THEY CARE ABOUT IS THEMSELVES.

Do you hate me yet? I'm sorry we had to end our relationship like this.

Moving on.

You might be wondering:

Giving!? What are some ways to give to people you meet, people you want to stay in touch with, and people you want to form new relationships with?

There are SOOO many ways you can give:

- Send them an article that they would enjoy reading based on their interests

- Send them a book recommendation that you think they would really like.

- Send them an email just letting them know that you're thinking of them

- Send them an introduction to someone they HAVE to meet

Giving is the new receiving. Kind of. When you give, SOOO many things will come back to you.

You might also be thinking:

"Well Tam, if all I do is give, give, and give, I'll never get anything for myself!!!"

Read the story with the farmers again above. Now I'll repeat this sentence again:

NO ONE CARES ABOUT YOU. ALL THEY CARE ABOUT IS THEMSELVES.

I'll repeat it 3 more times:

NO ONE CARES ABOUT YOU. ALL THEY CARE ABOUT IS THEMSELVES.

NO ONE CARES ABOUT YOU. ALL THEY CARE ABOUT IS THEMSELVES.

NO ONE CARES ABOUT YOU. ALL THEY CARE ABOUT IS THEMSELVES.

Got it? :)

The point of giving is to be a human being and simply help other people. Even when nothing might ever come back to you. That's the BEST secret to success.

"Because the truth is, people like people. We're wired for it. And people do business with other people. So when you learn to generally give to those people without expecting them to do something in return, you win. You'll perceive the world differently, and if we're being honest, be a better person because of it."

- Gary Vaynerchuk

Give, give, give, and you will receive.

This is the magic rule of life. I can't explain how it works but it just does. Some people have defined it as the Law of Reciprocity.

As psychologist Robert Cialdini (the author of *Influence*) puts it:

"The rule of reciprocity says that we should try to repay what another person has provided us. By virtue of the rule, we are obligated to the future repayment of favors, gifts, invitations, and the like.

The impressive aspect of the rule for reciprocation and the sense of obligation that goes with it is its pervasiveness in human culture. It is so widespread that after intensive study, sociologists such as Alvin Gouldner can report that there is no human society that does not subscribe to the rule"

When you network, it's not about you and what you want. Just imagine a stranger in front of you at Starbucks offers to pay for your drink.

"Wow, she is so sweet!", you automatically think. If she asked you for a favor, would you help her out?

If you're not a selfish person, you'd be much more willing to help her because she helped you. You actually feel slightly obligated to return the favor... and that's how it can be for networking. It's that simple.

The most successful people got to where they are because they give, CONSTANTLY.

Trust in others. Trust life. Trust me.

Be the special few that think about other people first and the benefits will be astronomical.

"You can have everything in life you want, if you will just help other people get what they want."

- *Zig Ziglar*

The Silver Bullet

I want to share with you ONE technique that has worked SOOOOoooo well for me... Yes, it involves giving.

The MOST EFFECTIVE thing that you can give to somebody is IDEAS.

Because for most people, they don't give a shit about coffee. There's going to be five college students cold emailing a business executive asking for coffee. This business executive probably makes 6 figures a year... They don't need some teenager buying them coffee.

So why the hell do people ALWAYS ASK PROFESSIONALS FOR COFFEE!?

You have to offer something of greater value. Money can work but it doesn't show that you have put any effort, time, and thought into your gift.

This is why IDEAS are the ultimate currency.

I wanted to get to know Yahya Bakka, one of the top youth speakers in the nation. I don't know what he charges for his 1-on-1 coaching program, but talking to some random kid like me... is not on his priority list.

I asked myself: How can I connect with Yahya?

I want to learn from him because he is twenty steps ahead of me in the career path that I want to go into. Instead of thinking... How can I get Yahya's attention? I switched my mindset to, How can I make this guy say **thank you** to me?

How can I give him something of such great value to the point where he would actually want to talk to me?

I went on his YouTube channel and saw that he made a video about rebranding his business. Yahya wanted to focus his attention on fitness and motivation instead of some of the work he was already doing… So a spark hit me.

I did my research. Because of my marketing background, I sent him 10 ideas on how he can help rebrand his YouTube channel. It took me 2 hours to understand what he was doing, where he was at, and where he was trying to go. It took me another hour to create 13 ideas specifically for his business.

Here's the email I sent him:

13 Free Ideas to Grow Your Audience on YouTube

Tam Pham <writetotampham@gmail.com>

to yahya

Hi Yahya,

This is Tam from Grant Baldwin's Facebook group, Booked & Paid to Speak. After talking to you more about your life goals and YouTube channel, I have few ideas that might be able to help you out.

1) Reddit

When you post quality content on very specific subreddits like bodybuilding, powerlifting, fitness, etc. you tend to pick up a lot of different new fans.

2) Quora

Although you said your writing is not your strong suit, you can go the extra mile and record a video specific to the Quora question and post it on YouTube at the same time!

Once you're considered a thought leader on Quora, people naturally start going to your site and there have been many instances where people get hired for coaching, consulting, etc.

Quora also works with the upvoting system, similar to Reddit.

3) Partner up with other YouTubers

It's a win-win situation when you make videos with other YouTubers. They can be from fitness like Mike Chang (SixPackShortcuts) or Bart Kwan etc.

You're an excellent performer. Have you ever considered doing comedy skits with people who share the target demographic? Tim Ferriss, Simple Pickup, JustKiddingFilms, David So Comedy, etc.)

Pro tip: Instead of asking them if you can be a guest in their channel. Invite them to do a video with you! Send them over a video script or 10 video ideas just to show them how serious you are.

4) Guest post on Fitness Blogs

Like the example with Quora, you can make above and beyond to create a personalized video for a fitness blog answering a very specific question. Guest posts have to be extraordinary and compelling. You got this :)

5) Start making fitness products

I was on your website and I've noticed your two different products targeting teens. Since you plan on making the transition to coaching, hosting seminars and conferences, etc. it would be wise to work on products (or more videos) targeting where you want to go.

6) Start a fitness meetup group... or join one!

There's nothing better than an in-person community. Build trust and healthy relationships with other fitness enthusiasts :)

7) Create tutorial videos

A create formula I've studied is: How to [Action] with [Something] in [Duration]

For example .

- How to [Tone your back?] with [Dead Lifts] in [3 weeks]
- How to [Do A Complete Biceps Workout] with [No Weights] in [15 minutes]
- How to [Run A Marathon] with [No prior Experience] in [90 days]

8) Go straight to the source

Go directly to athletic teams in high school or college and offer to do some special workshops with them. Whatever part of fitness you specialize in, come in and have a day dedicated to increasing that skill. Impress the coaches and fitness instructors with your high energy. At most colleges, there are even organizations dedicated to fitness or bodybuilding. Get in touch with the president in charge to come and give a guest talk. Sure this doesn't scale, but it's a great start to this newer transition that you are aiming for.

9) Be very specific with your market

I understand how much you want to impact people's lives but ages 15-35 can be a bit wide.

One market that I can definitely see you doing is targeting professionals who don't have enough time or knowledge to work out properly. They can be seen as successful entrepreneurs, top-level executives, etc. Just an idea!

10) Podcast tour

In text form:

"Hi Yahya,

After talking to you more about your life goals and YouTube channel, I have few ideas that might be able to help you out.

1) Reddit

When you post quality content on very specific subreddits like bodybuilding, powerlifting, fitness,

etc. you tend to pick up a lot of different new fans.

2) Quora

Although you said your writing is not your strong suit, you can go the extra mile and record a video specific to the Quora question and post it on YouTube at the same time!

29

Once you're considered a thought leader on Quora, people naturally start going to your site and there have been many instances where people get hired for coaching, consulting, etc.

Quora also works with the upvoting system, similar to Reddit

3) Partner up with other YouTubers

It's a win-win situation when you make videos with other YouTubers. They can be from Fitness like Mike Chang (SixPackShortcuts) or Bart Kwan etc.

You're an excellent performer. Have you ever considered doing comedy skits with people who share the target demographic? Tim Ferriss, Simple Pickup, JustKiddingFilms, David So Comedy, etc.)

Pro tip: Instead of asking them if you can be a guest in their channel, invite them over to do a video with you! Send them over a video script or 10 video ideas just to show them how serious you are.

4) Guest post on Fitness Blogs

Like the example with Quora, you can make above and beyond to create a personalized video for a fitness blog answering a very specific question. Guest posts have to be extraordinary and compelling. You got this :)

5) Start making fitness products

I was on your website and I've noticed your two different products targeting teens. Since you plan on making the transition to coaching, hosting seminars and conferences, etc. it would be wise to work on products (or more videos) targeting where you want to go.

6) Start a fitness meetup group... or join one!

There's nothing better than an in-person community. Build trust and healthy relationships with other fitness enthusiasts :)

7) Create tutorial videos

A create formula I've studied is: How to [Action] with [Something] in [Duration]

For example...

- *How to [Tone your back] with [Dead Lifts] in [3 weeks]*

- *How to [Do A Complete Biceps Workout] with [No Weights] in [15 minutes]*

- *How to [Run A Marathon] with [No prior Experience] in [90 days]*

8) Go straight to the source

Go directly to athletic teams in high school or college and offer to do some special workshops with them. Whatever part of fitness you specialize in, come in and have a day dedicated to increasing that skill. Impress the coaches and fitness instructors with your high energy and knowledge... this might be your foot in the door for other opportunities!

At most colleges, there are even organizations dedicated to fitness or bodybuilding. Get in touch with the president in charge to come and give a guest talk. Sure this doesn't scale, but it's a great start to this newer transition that you are aiming for.

9) Be very specific with your market

I understand how much you want to impact people's lives but ages 16-35 can be a bit wide.

One market that I can definitely see you doing is targeting professionals who don't have enough time or knowledge to work out properly. They can be seen as successful entrepreneurs, top-level executives, etc. Just an idea!

10) Podcast tour

You have a great gift of communication. Share it with the world through other people's podcast!

Everyone wants to get fit and have a better life. Target the podcasts who are all about self-improvement and inspiration. Become a fan first and introduce yourself to the host. Build a relationship, plant this seed, and maybe you can become a guest? Jab jab jab right hook ;-)

Maybe even talk to Grant Baldwin! Although he did have another youth speaker, Josh Shipp, on his podcast already. But you can ask to talk about your next goals (fitness, seminars, conferences)

11) Instagram

Instagram, out of all the social networks, is HUGE on fitness. Showcase some quick words of wisdom, videos of you working out, and refer people back to your YouTube channel.

12) Fitness Expos

I haven't personally explored this path but my friends say this is a chance to meet people in this space and get exposed to many different organizations. Worth a shot? Maybe? :)

13) Bonus Idea: Have your own apparel

This is farther down the path but you can really build a brand behind your fitness track. Once people are wearing your swag, it'll be a constant advertisement. Plus, it'll make a great gift :)

Although not all of these ideas are super great, I hope you found at least one or two of them to be useful. Let me know if you need any clarity on my ideas. Since I'm in your target market, I'll be happy to answer some questions if you'd like!

Talk to you soon!

Best,

Tam"

Look how detailed this email is!!! You know what happened next? Immediate response. Why?

Because I never asked for anything. Yahya can SEE how much effort I put in and he's thinking to himself, "This guy knows what he's talking about."

And you want to know what happened?

He offered ME a free 30 minute Skype session to talk about whatever I wanted... an opportunity that my broke ass could never afford.

WOW.

We ended up having a great conversation and our relationship started off beautifully.

So I started writing ideas for so many different people. Including James Altucher, famous entrepreneur, investor, and author.

I gave an idea to James on how to increase the attendance for his meetup groups. He took my idea, used it, and the online community gained 2,000 members. The in-person communities tripled in size if not more... in less than 72 hours. It was absolutely insane!

With ideas, I'm no longer the pesky kid that wants to take them out for coffee. I understand them, have a genuine desire in helping them, and have the ability to form a much stronger relationship. I bet you if I emailed James or Yahya right now, they would respond immediately.

Now giving ideas doesn't just have to be with high level people. This applies with EVERYONE.

Just recently:

- I gave my friend 10 ideas for topics she could write about for her new blog.

- I gave my friend 10 ideas on how to get himself known as a photographer.

- I gave my co-worker 10 ideas on how he can be more productive.

- I gave 10 ideas to a person on Quora answering a question about college.

- I gave 10 ideas to a friend on how to market his new app.

Just imagine that you're trying to strengthen your network (how did I know that?).

What if your friend took the time to give you 10 ideas on some networking strategies you can implement, organizations you can get involved with, or programs that you should look out for...? How would that make you feel?

Happy? Grateful? Appreciative? Do you have a natural feeling that you want to help them out as well?

Ideas WORK. Ideas are the new currency. Ideas > Money

Will it work all the time? No. Like anything else in life, nothing is guaranteed.

Will this approach be more beneficial than asking for coffee? Hell yes.

How do you get started?

ACTION: Write 10 ideas a day. About anything.

- 10 ideas on how to be more grateful in life

- 10 ideas on new businesses to start

- 10 ideas on blog posts you can write

- 10 ideas on how to get more active

- 10 ideas how to become more organized

In the beginning, most of your ideas will be bad. That's a given and don't be discouraged. **The point is not about the ideas themselves yet... but that you are exercising the idea muscle.** When you regularly exercise that idea muscle, you can become an IDEA MACHINE: Coming up with ideas for anything on the spot.

When your idea muscle gets stronger, you can send your ideas to people you really want to get to know.

- 10 ideas to Tim Ferriss (Famous Author, Entrepreneur, & Investor) on guests he should interview for his podcast

- 10 ideas to Michelle Phan (Makeup Artist & YouTube Celebrity) on how to improve her YouTube channel

- 10 ideas to Hoodie Allen (Badass Rapper) on new t-shirt designs he should sell

- 10 ideas to John Lee Dumas (Podcast King) on how he can take his business to the next level

- 10 ideas to Ryan Hoover (Startup Founder) on new features he can use for his product.

Some of them won't respond, it's okay. Don't be mad or feel like you're doing something wrong. **The moment you expect something in return is the moment when you're doomed for failure.**

Remember the previous chapter? GIVE GIVE GIVE. For those who do respond, it'll be so worth it.

When you're at a networking event and you listen to some of the challenges the other person is facing in their business, give them ideas on the spot. Why?

It shows that you care and that you want to help. You're not paying them money to be your friend… but showing your appreciation through genuine thought.

I do have to warn you that when you give ideas, do so appropriately. Don't blurt them out mid conversation and expect them to love you right on the spot.

Let's say I'm talking to Jane and she tells me that she is struggling to gain traffic to her fitness blog. Instead of saying mid conversation…

"Jane, why the hell haven't you used YouTube as a medium!?!?!"

"Jane, have you seriously never heard of Reddit?! There are tons of Fitness communities on there alone."

"Jane, do you even have an email list!? You have to start building it. NOW."

That situation can get ugly REAL QUICK. Try this approach:

"So Jane, what have you tried so far? What is working and what isn't?"

You are listening and understanding more. Then after you have a better knowledge of her business, then you can suggest some ideas.

"Have you considered using Reddit as a traffic generator?

I've personally discovered many fitness experts on Reddit and it's something that you might be interested in. If so, I'll be happy to walk you through how it works!"

Notice the difference in approaches? One is demanding and condescending. The other is much more understanding and gentle.

Give ideas away and do so respectfully, don't be a show it off know it all :)

Action: Write 10 ideas a day to strengthen the idea muscle and give ideas to other people. FOR FREE.

You might also be thinking:

"Tam… why don't I charge for my ideas? It takes time and effort to create ideas, it doesn't make sense to give it out for free."

Remember what Gary Vaynerchuk said earlier? It's so important that I'll bring it up again:

"Because the truth is, people like people. We're wired for it. And people do business with other people. So when you learn to generally give to those people without expecting them to do something in return, you win. You'll perceive the world differently, and if we're being honest, be a better person because of it."

- Gary Vaynerchuk

If there is one thing in this whole book that you take away, I hope it's this:

GIVE, GIVE, GIVE. And you shall receive.

Ideas are one of the best ways to give to people.

GIVING is how you genuinely connect with people. Never expect anything in return. This is how you truly win.

Make Them Feel Important

We all have this friend named Stephanie where she does ALL of the talking… Whenever you would mention ANYTHING… She would instantly cut you off.

Like,

Me: "Yeah, that reminds me of the time where I went to that restaurant with my family! My favorite dish was..."

Stephanie: *"YEAH THAT RESTAURANT WAS SO GOOD. Did you try the lobster pizza?"*

Me: "No... I haven't but I hear..."

Stephanie: *"O M G it's soooooo good. You have to try it!!! Anyways, back to me."*

No matter what story you bring up, Stephanie will always brings it back to herself.

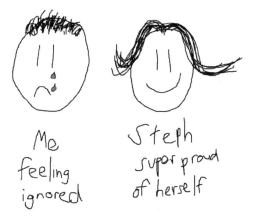

Me
feeling
ignored

Steph
super proud
of herself

When you are in a future conversation, don't be a Stephanie. You make other people feel insignificant. If I could sum up the classic book, *How To Win Friends And Influence People by Dale Carnegie,* in one sentence, it would be this:

MAKE THE OTHER PERSON FEEL IMPORTANT

This works wonders. Pretty corny but this is why we have two ears and one mouth: To listen.

Or when you're on a date, listen more than you speak.

When you're talking to your grandparents, look them in their eyes and simply listen.

If you haven't noticed at this stage in your life...people LOOOOOOOOVVVEEE talking about themselves. It's not because people are arrogant or cocky, it's because they want that feeling of importance. It is something ALL humans crave.

So when you're networking, ALWAYS make the other person feel important.

How?

- Have your full attention on them (put away your damn phone!)

- Keep good eye contact

- Nod to acknowledge their points (but not every other second... you'll look like a pup desperate for food)

- DO NOT THINK OF YOUR NEXT RESPONSE UNTIL AFTER THEY FINISH TALKING. The moment you do that, it is the biggest indicator that you are not FULLY listening to them.

- Be fully engaged and present in the moment

There are so many more ways but I don't want to overwhelm you with the little details. I highly recommend reading, _How To Win Friends And Influence People by Dale Carnegie_ for more information. But the bigger picture is this = MAKE THEM FEEL IMPORTANT.

I have a challenge for you for the next time you "network."

How can you make whoever you're talking to feel like they're the MOST IMPORTANT person in the world?

Bill Clinton does a fantastic job at this. People say that when they talk to him, he makes them feel so special. Like an angel. Even his opponents would admit that about the extremely charismatic Bill Clinton.

The moment you make others feel important is the moment where everyone will love you, trust you, and respect you.

This applies to when you're at a business conference, in school, or even with your family. Humans crave the feeling of importance... so give it to them!

In your next conversation with your sibling, friend, or co-worker... try this one technique out: **How can you make them feel important?**

Drop Your Agenda

I have this friend named Curtis and he comes to every event with an agenda.

Curtis makes a list of people that he HAS to meet, usually the top speakers in the event. And he will stop at nothing until he connects with them. Do you see the problem?

Put this book down and take a second to think of what is wrong with Curtis's way of thinking

*

*

*

*

*

*

*

The answer: By having such a strict agenda, you're not OPEN to other opportunities. By only focusing on the top dogs (high level speakers), you will feel less inclined to talk to anyone else. More times than not, you won't even get to connect with these speakers because EVERYONE has the same agenda as you.

So just drop it.

Aim to connect but don't make it your sole purpose. Be open

to the people sitting next to you, the woman in front of you waiting for lunch, the man chilling by himself in the corner.

There's no such thing as a useless person.

Everyone is unique in their own way. Don't be blind and narrow minded when it comes to meeting people. You seriously never know who you'll meet, so be open to everything.

Many people come to events only looking for "relevant" people but that is so full of BS. I know of people who go to events exclusively to meet others in a certain field, like Bitcoin. But just because I'm not into Bitcoin does NOT mean I'm going to treat the other person like shit.

I have a friend who is working on a startup to revolutionize the sperm bank industry. Pretty random right?

Although I have no interest in the sperm bank industry, I treated him with respect and the utmost kindness. I listened to him and his vision. I learned new things and gained a new friend.

Now guess what?

I still keep in touch with him. In fact, we ate sushi the other day. Why?

Because he is genuinely a cool dude... We talk about business, books, even girls. He's a close mentor with everything I'm doing, including this book. So is he "relevant"? You could argue no when I first met him.

Me + Sperm Banks? Not a lethal combination.

But we're awesome friends and we are able to learn a lot from each other.

In general, never count anyone out. You seriously never know what kind of connections you will develop. So drop your agenda, be open to all the possibilities, and have fun!

Your ABC's

questi

This is how networking usually works in most ~ settings.

Say Doobs meets Kat and she asks, "What do you do?"

Doobs: "I run a software development company that revolutionizes the way small business interacts with hardware companies who also work with our technology team to work on our secret project ISUCK."

Kat: "Ah, that's so interesting." (trying not to fall asleep)

Doobs: "So what do you do?"

Kat: "I run an ad agency to help entrepreneurs market to their target audience and grow revenue, increase brand awareness, and up their sales."

Doobs: "Ah, that's so interesting"

Kat: "Well, here's my card. It was great to meet you."

Doobs: "You too."

ZZZZZZZZzzzzzzzzzzzzzzzzz..................

HOW BORRRRRIIIIINNNGGGGGGG......

You'd be surprised how many of these conversations I overhear. Even when they a ridiculously boring business, one thing you HAVE to learn and practice is to be genuinely curious.

When you are genuinely curious, you're able to ask better

/ons like…

"So what has been the biggest challenge for your company thus far?"

- "Who are some clients that you have been working with? And how is that going?"

- "Is there any way that I can help?"

Remember the golden rule to networking? Make them feel important. Here's another thing you should remember: ABC. Do you remember your ABC's?

Yes, it means: Always Be Curious.

LET THEM DO THE TALKING and always be curious. By being curious, you never stop asking questions and are always willing to learn.

The moment you STOP being curious is the moment you stop caring. There is ALWAYS something you can learn, you can help with, or have a moment of happiness :)

Remember, people looOoOoOoovvvvvee talking about themselves so listen in, make them feel important, and always be curious.

- Be curious to what they're up to.

- Be curious on their background.

- Be curious on where they grew up at.

- Be curious on what books they read.

- Be curious on who they admire as role models.

You never know how much you have in common with somebody until you are curious.

Next time you go anywhere, never forget your ABC's.

Be interesting

There's always this guy named Rob who goes to every freaking networking event.

Literally every conference, meet up, or summit... Rob is there tweeting away.

When you see him, it's no surprise.

"Hey Rob, how's it going!?"

"Good Tam, nice to see you again!!!"

Every time I see a Rob, I'm always working on a new project. My first projects failed, my next ones were thrown out, and the current one is usually in development.

Rob is different.

Rob is never working on anything.

Rob is the kind of person who would ask high level people to get coffee, just to talk.

Rob is the kind of person who would learn so much from people and the events he attends... but never actually does anything.

Rob is the kind of person who spends more time tweeting motivational quotes than creating anything of real value.

In short, Rob is uninteresting...

You have to have some kind of reason where people would DESIRE to talk to you. Now I know it's never about you... but you have to be somewhat interesting.

You can't just be a floater at every event for no reason.

When I was working on my first business, some people would be extremely interested in what I was doing. Others would be more curious about my entrepreneurship journey. Some might really dig my mission in what I'm trying to accomplish.

This gives people a reason to:

- keep in touch with me

- pick my brain

- help and support me

- connect me to somebody

- give me advice

When they meet Rob... they get a cool business card but there's no solid reason to keep in constant contact with him.

He's working on nothing… why would anyone follow up with Rob? Imagine what that email might look like:

"Hey Rob,

It was great meeting you at the event yesterday. Good luck with nothing!

Best,

Tam"

L O L

What is my advice to you?

BE INTERESTING!

Do cool stuff like:

- Work on a project

- Start a blog

- Write a book

- Film a documentary

- Interview guests on a podcast

- Start a business

- Learn new skills

- Make videos for YouTube

All of these things (and many other activities) can easily be learned online through YouTube, Blogs, & Podcasts. You can even go take online courses on Udemy and Coursera to learn more on how to get started in any of these activities.

I remember when I first started networking; I would be honest and say,

"Hey! I'm a student trying to learn more about stocks and investing. Do you mind if I ask you a quick question about it?"

The person would say, "Sure!"

And they would give me some advice or teach me something new. They feel important because they have the power and the position to help me. I now can use their solid advice and have a reason to keep in touch with them.

I always try to find some sort of connection with them. For example, if the other person loves to write, then I try to find ways to talk about my blog. Or if the other person wants to start a podcast some day, I can tell them about my podcast and help them get started in the right steps.

You get the point.

Even when you're working on nothing at the moment, don't be a Rob. Have something worth talking about! Make it easy and give people a chance to genuinely connect with you!

Be interesting.

Ask Better Questions

You want to know what the most common questions asked during networking events are?

#1 - What do you do?

#2 - Who do you know here?

#3 - What brought you here?

All decent conversations starters but...

ZZZZZZZZZzzzzz......

BORRRRRRIIIInnnnnggggg....

When you ask these questions, YOU WILL BE LIKE EVERYONE ELSE. People ask these questions so often that people have MEMORIZED ELEVATOR SCRIPTS FOR THESE.

Including me, and I didn't even try to memorize it. Bummer.

So, what is the solution?

ASK BETTER QUESTIONS

You want to ask questions that catch the other person off guard (in a good way) and allow them to open up a side that most people don't see.

Real life Example:

Me: "Hey, my name is Tam"

Jack: "Hey, my name is Jack."

Me: "Jack, I have a question for you. What do you do for fun?"

Jack's business poker face instantly melts away. He starts telling me ALL about his dreams of becoming a musician and performer. I could literally see Jack's eyes LIGHT UP when he's talking about what he was SOOOO passionate about.

Then our conversations transitions into dreams, music, performance, old stories from parties, and so much more.

And guess what?

When Jack goes home today and goes through all the business cards he received... he will NEVER forget the person who he really hit it off with. That memory will be the highlight of the whole day.

Moral of the story? Ask better questions.

Try to ask questions that gets them OUT OF THEIR OWN PERSONA.

Questions like:

1) What is your dream?

2) What would you do with a billion dollars?

3) Where were you born?

4) If you could live anywhere in the world, where would that be?

5) What are some of your favorite books?

6) Who are some of your inspirations?

7) What do you like to do on the weekends?

8) What's one thing that you would do if you knew you could not fail?

9) How's your day going?

10) What is some advice you would tell your teenage self?

Because of this, you both can start a much more in-depth and awesome conversation. You're able to really connect with them on a much deeper level than being strictly business related.

Remember, people LOVE talking about themselves... so let them. Listen closely, be curious, and keep the conversation going.

The point of networking is to be friends!!! Friends will naturally love, support, and want to help you. Never forget that.

Find that connection you share with the other person and have great conversations. Also remember that people are human beings... not just factory workers with one job in life.

Don't be like 90% of people who ask the same questions over and over. It gets boring and repetitive. Be different. Be unique. And most importantly...

Ask better questions.

All about the Conversation

A dating coach asked a room full of women if they ever had this thought:

"If a man really wanted to meet you, then he would have had the balls to walk up to you already."

90% of the women raised their hands.

Let's pause for a moment.

Does anyone realize how STUPID this sounds? A man sees an average of 30 attractive people a day (living in the city).

     1) He's not going to approach all 30 women.

     2) Not all men are super extroverted.

     3) Men are afraid of rejection and pressure.

Men are human beings too!

So when a woman is with her friend standing in front of Starbucks minding their own business, a man is thinking...

"Wow, she is the prettiest girl I've ever seen... I don't want to approach her and ask her out though. She's with her friend; she might have a boyfriend and reject me, or something."

The women is thinking,

"Wow this guy is glancing at me for the past 2 minutes but isn't even going to approach me. He's probably not the one."

There are two sides to every story. Is this a book about dating? No, I'm probably not qualified to write that.

This chapter is all about conversation. Don't think of networking like asking someone out. There's so much pressure and rejection involved... Instead, just start a causal conversation.

The key here is START.

No one is asking you to have a super deep conversation with anyone. Just start the conversation and see where it goes. And don't be afraid because people go to places for many different reasons:

- People go to Starbucks for the coffee (or for the Instagram picture).

- People go to parties to TURN UP WITH COOL PEOPLE.

- People go to networking events to MEET AWESOME PEOPLE.

Everyone at your next social event will have the same fears as you:

1) No one is going to talk to me

2) I won't make any friends

3) I'm going to be super lonely

YOU have to take the initiative and approach somebody. Just start a normal conversation and the other person would be soooo grateful :)

Starting a conversation is different from asking someone out on the first move.

We're entering a no pressure, low-risk thing here. Remember the better questions we talked about? Use them!

Just start a conversation and let things flow naturally :)

Be a fan first

I wanted to get to know Ryan Porter, who is a kick ass motivational speaker and an awesome dude, but I didn't know where I should start.

I saw his TEDx video and was super impressed at him and his company. So I sent him an email saying how much I loved his work.

I even tweeted and asked, "Why haven't you blown up yet!?"

He humbly replied to me through Twitter. Ryan was also super responsive through email even though I never met him. Why?

Imagine if someone compliments you. How would you feel? How might you feel towards that person?

For me, I always feel so awesome. How do I feel about that person? I think that they are so brave & kind for letting me know what they think. I automatically think that they're awesome!!!

So if you want to meet anyone high-level or even on your level, BE A FAN FIRST.

Don't think like you're sucking up to them... you are giving them genuine compliments that you dig their work. What's vile about that?

Be a fan.

As a blogger and YouTuber, I get so excited when I see engagement on my content. When someone types a super detailed comment on my YouTube video complimenting me on my work, I WILL remember that.

When someone comments on my blog and asks me a super thoughtful question, I WILL remember that.

When someone emails me ten reasons on how my blog has helped them, I WILL remember that.

Remember the law of reciprocity? Now I'm so much more likely to engage with them and maybe even help them in their endeavors. I've helped many different people because of this sole reason... They were unselfish first... constantly giving. Then they ask for a small favor when they need it most, and I'll be happy to oblige.

Support people in their endeavors. Give them ideas. Share their work. Only after being a fan is when you ask for anything.

Follow Up

Imagine Joe goes to a party and he meets a really cute girl. They really hit it off! They end up talking about work, their families, and spend the rest of the night talking about life.

She made Joe really happy.

As the night winds down, it's time to depart. Joe gives her his phone number and he tells her to call him tomorrow to hang out again.

"Will do!" She says.

A day goes by, no phone call yet. Two days go by, not even a text message from her. A week later, Joe is at another party checking his phone every other minute but still, no response.

She never followed up :(

If you were Joe, how would this make you feel?

Whenever you meet anybody... YOU have to be the one to follow up. This is a mistake that 75% of people make when they network (Again, another made-up statistic to emphasize my point).

This mistake is so costly!!!

What did Joe do wrong here? He left the power in HER hands. Next time, Joe should get HER number and HE should be the one calling. Why?

Because he is the 25% that will actually follow up.

Following up is a SKILL and most people don't do it. When you go to your next party, event, or social... YOU have to be in power. Take their business card. Jot their email address down. Save their phone number. Then YOU follow up with them... This is so crucial.

Why should you even follow up?

- Future Collaboration

- Stay in touch

- Chance for you to give, give, give

- Be updated & connected

- Get to know your new friend on a deeper level

How should you follow up?

Make it a very simple message. For a business networking purposes, a follow up might look like this:

"Hi [NAME],

I had a great time connecting with you at [EVENT]! It was really cool to talk to you about [TOPIC 1], [TOPIC 2], & [TOPIC 3].

You mentioned how much you loved [SOMETHING], so I wanted to give you [GIFT] that I came across early this morning! Hope this helps and let's definitely stay in touch.

Best,

[NAME]"

Let's break this down... What did we do right?

1) We established where we met

2) I listed things we talked about which tells them that I was paying attention

3) I remembered they loved something in particular so I want to give, give, give them a little something. Could be articles, book recommendation, or even an offer to introduce them to someone.

4) Don't ask for anything BIG. Plant the seed and let it blossom naturally.

5) "Let's stay in touch" BAM. Great ending :) When appropriate, you can change this follow up to ask for lunch, coffee, or a phone call!

In short, don't forget to follow up and don't be a Joe!

In a social setting, send them a text at the very least. The point is that after you meet an amazing person that you really got along with, why stop the conversation there?

Follow up with everyone you want to stay in touch with... Never forget.

Make It A Habit

Throughout the whole book, we have really learned what networking really is and how powerful it can be. How do you take it to the next step?

Make it a habit! How?

Do it every day.

Do what?

Dun dun dun...

GIVING.

Here's what I want you to do RIGHT NOW:

1) Make a list of the people you want to keep in touch with or want to know better. About 50 people should be good enough.

2) Number them from #1 - 25 (Order doesn't matter)

3) Every day, give to at least one person. After #25, rinse & repeat. (Feel free to add more people as time goes on)

Remember all of the stuff you can give?

An article, introduction, book recommendation, a thank you, or simply a "just thinking about you" email.

Remember the 10 ideas!?!? That's the silver bullet!

Remember how humans crave the feeling of importance? Give that to them as well!

Remember the law of reciprocity? The more you help, the more willing they will help you.

Remember being curious? Ask them how they're doing and offer ways where you can help.

Remember how you should be a fan first? Comment on their blog. Compliment them on their new website design. Publically share their work.

Invest in your network.

Doing these kinds of exercises every day actually feels really good. At the end of the day, you can say you successfully helped someone and put genuine thought into your efforts.

Watch all of the remarkable feedback you will get! YOU will be among the select few who finally understands networking

BONUS: Take it a step further. What I do personally is whenever I feel like it (usually once every few weeks), I post a Facebook status:

Tam Pham
· 30 October 2014

devoting 1 hour to helping anybody with ANYTHING starting..... now! ask away 👍 (i'm actually serious, let me help you)

Share · Buffer · 👍 39 💬 27

Then, I can help out anyone that asks through messages, phone call, or Skype. It's such a great feeling to help people and they are extremely appreciative for it.

James Altucher does a Q&A session every Thursday on Twitter... helping hundreds of people instantly every week.

Many successful entrepreneurs and authors hosts AMA's (Ask Me Anything) on Reddit to help anyone that needs it.

My friend & successful entrepreneur, Scott Oldford, has all of his Wednesday blocked off with 15 minute phone calls with anyone who wants to connect. From 7am - 7pm, he's simply helping people one by one.

You don't have to go as extreme as Scott... But all of the best leaders and most successful people GIVE, and they make it a habit. **Will you be next?**

REJECTION

I'm going to tell you something that no one has the guts to tell you.

Not everyone is going to want to be your friend.

No matter how curious you are. No matter how important you make them feel. No matter how much you listen to their boring business... Not everyone is going to like you.

Let me tell you all the possible scenarios that could happen:

1) You walk up to them and they give you a weird look like, "Who are you and why are you talking to me?"

2) You follow up with somebody through email and they never get back to you

3) You try to join a group of people but no one opens up the circle for you

4) You try to talk to somebody and they don't even look up and acknowledge you

5) You notice their fake smiles and strong body language that they don't want to talk to you.

Is the problem you? No, it's not. For these situations, don't sweat. Like how YOU are very selective with your friends, they might be too.

Or maybe they don't have enough time to respond to your email. Or maybe they're having a bad day. Or maybe something horrible just happened to them and they're not in a mood to talk.

Never assume that anyone hates you right off the bat. Someone is always fighting an unseen battle. Don't let these situations get to you and simply move on.

Provide support when appropriate but overall, be okay with not everyone wanting to be your friend. You can only do so much...

Be okay with possible rejection. It's going to happen. It has happened to me a countless number of times, and I'm still standing.

It is OKAY.

There are literally millions of other people you can meet. Don't sweat the small stuff :)

Final Thoughts

Networking = making friends. Your networking skills do not just "turn on" at a conference. We practice networking every day. You can meet some AMAZING people on the streets on New York, the person behind you on the grocery store, the cute girl sitting next to you in class. You never know who you'll meet. But I hope you've learned a few takeaways:

1) Networking = Friends

Think of networking like making friends. It's supposed to be fun, helpful, and awesome :)

2) Start with YOU

Be authentic in everything that you do.

3) Decide that you will be a superb networker

All we have is decision. DECIDE right now that you will be a great networker and all of the smaller details will follow.

4) Know your WHY

Have a strong reason on why you want to build your network. Whenever you're feeling lost or confused, always refer back to your WHY.

5) Get into the mindset of GIVING

Give, give, give and you shall receive. It's the magic rule of life!

6) Give your ideas away for FREE

Write 10 ideas every day. Practice your idea muscle. Give your ideas for free to people you want to get to know. Rinse and repeat.

7) Make them feel important

All humans crave the feeling of importance. So give it to them!

8) ABC: Always Be Curious

The moment you stop being curious is the moment you stop being interested in the other person. Never forget your ABC's!

9) Drop Your Agenda

The moment you have a strict agenda is the moment when you're too closed to meeting anyone else. Be open. See new opportunities in everything that you do.

10) Be interesting

Do something cool like a podcast, business, or a blog. Or simply wanting to learn more about a particular subject. Don't be a floater!

11) Ask better questions

99% of starter questions are boOoOorrring. Be the 1% that actually some awesome questions.

12) Start a convo

Remember, you're not asking anyone out! All you're doing is just starting a conversation. Just do it :)

13) Be a fan first

Support other people in your space and naturally, they will want to support you. Win-win!

14) Follow Up

Always be in control. Take down their business card, email address, or phone number… and follow up!

15) Make Networking + Giving a habit

Give any way that you can, all the time. Make it a habit!

There are all the secrets that I wished I had five years ago and I really hope that you use what you've learned and become a networking success story.

Download the FREE Networking Checklist:

www.TamPham.co/NetworkingBonus

Save this guide to your computer, hang it up on your wall, or event share it with your friends!

The Time Is Now!

Congrats! You have just learned all of the untold secrets about networking and I'm so excited for you.

Use this book as a reference before you go to any future events and I promise you that you will be able to connect to so many more people. If you practice these techniques consistently, you will make so many more connections, have access to more opportunities than you can handle, and achieve your goals faster with a stronger support system.

The time is NOW for you to go out in the real world and take ACTION! As an appreciation gift to you, I created a print out of the book's main point that you can stick on your wall or have with you before you go to your next event.

Download the FREE Networking Checklist: www.TamPham.co/NetworkingBonus

Stay awesome :)

Sincerely,

Tam Pham

Recommended Resources

For additional reading on networking, please check out these awesome resources. Highly recommend!

Book: The Trusted Advisor - Robert Galford

Book: Never Eat Alone - Keith Ferrazzi

Article: From Tim Ferriss To Seth Godin: How To Interview & Build Relationships With The Most "Influential" People In The World

Thank You

Before you go, I'd like to say "thank you" for purchasing my eBook.

I know you could have picked from dozens of books on networking. But you took a chance with my guide.

So a big thanks for downloading this book and reading all the way to the end. If you liked this book, then I need your help. Please take a moment to leave a review for this book on Amazon.

Pretty please? :)

This feedback will help me continue to write the kind of books that helps you gets results. Your review would be s0o0o appreciative :')

Contact

Whoever you are, I want to thank you for reading this book and I hope you got a lot out of it. If you want to get in touch, my email is "writetoTamPham@gmail.com." I personally read and respond to every email (I am not a robot!) So I would love to hear from you!

You can also tweet me (@MrTamPham). **Let's genuinely connect :-)**

Manufactured by Amazon.ca
Bolton, ON

23520150R00042